LIVING
the
DAYS
of
LENT

1999

Pages contributed by
the Sisters of Charity of Saint Elizabeth

Edited by Anita M. Constance, S.C.

Paulist Press
New York • Mahwah, N.J.

Unless otherwise noted, all scripture quotations are from the *New Revised Standard Version of the Bible,* copyright © 1989 by the Division of Christian Education of the National Council of Churches of Christ in the U.S.A., and are used by permission. All rights reserved.

Copyright © 1998 by The Sisters of Charity of Saint Elizabeth.

All rights reserved. No part of this book may be reproduced or transmitted in any form or by any means, electronic or mechanical, including photocopying, recording or by any information storage and retrieval system without permission in writing from the Publisher.

ISBN: 0-8091-3839-5

Cover and book design by Saija Autrand.
Illustrations by Eileen Cantlin Verbus.

Published by Paulist Press
997 Macarthur Boulevard
Mahwah, New Jersey 07430

www.paulistpress.com

Printed and bound in the
United States of America

Introduction

Lent is a time for listening. It is not so much a time for thinking or doing as it is a time for reflection. Lent is a time for listening. It is a time to go to the sanctuary of our hearts and there, with Jesus, search the corners and shadows that will speak his word in ways we may never have heard before.

Lent is a time for listening. It is a time for resting in the life, passion and death of Jesus, to be shown a unique, personal path of discipleship. Lent is a time for listening. It is not a time for sacrifice or self-denial unless we hear those words within our hearts. It is not a time for almsgiving or self-giving unless we hear those words within our hearts. It is not a time for fasting or forgiveness unless we hear those words within our hearts.

Can we trust our hearts? Yes. Can we trust our inner ear? Yes. Why? Because the Word of God, Jesus Christ, is with us, within us, around us—at all times and for all time. All things were created through him. All things were created in him. He is for all and in all. Lent is a time for listening. . . . Trust your heart!

—Anita M. Constance, S.C.
Editor

February 17
Ash Wednesday

As a child I loved the Ash Wednesday readings, particularly the gospel. As one who abhorred the limelight, I heard the gospel as consoling to privacy. Growing from the concrete thinking of a child to the more abstract reasoning of an adult, I now hear a powerful call in today's readings.

Despite the outward sign of ashes on our foreheads, we are called today to turn our eyes inward for honest soul-searching. Ash Wednesday begins a holy season of forty days—a time to return to the Lord with our "whole heart." Today's scriptures ask us if our outer actions reflect our inner beliefs and vice versa.

Rather than finding consolation in the apparent affirmation of privacy in the gospel reading, we are challenged to consistency. Is my prayer reflected in my daily actions? Are my words consistent with my beliefs? Perhaps adjustments are needed so that "in him we might become the very holiness of God" (2 Cor 5:21 NAB).

I will listen to what I say today, and ask myself if my words are a reflection of my soul.

Readings: Joel 2:12-18; Psalms 51; 2 Corinthians 5:20–6:2; Matthew 6:1-6, 16-18

Thursday, February 18

"For those who want to save their life will lose it, and those who lose their life for my sake will find it." —Lk 9:24

Today's readings challenge us to be clear about our goal as we set out on our Lenten journey. Moses tells the Hebrew people on their desert journey:

> **Choose life so that you . . . may live.**
> —Dt 30:19

But today, what is the life we are to choose?

Our natural tendencies direct us to a life that is prosperous, blessed and long; and that is part of God's promise to us. But is this pleasant life, which nature desires, true life? The life God offers—God who is life—is a share in divine life, far beyond what any natural desire could envision . . . or reach.

We are challenged, in the book of Deuteronomy, to love God, walk in his ways, keep God's commands, hold fast. Jesus makes it even clearer: Deny yourself, take up your cross each day and follow me. At first this may seem contradictory to life, especially to our natural tendencies. But the life we lose is not our share in God's life. Life in God—worth infinitely more than the whole world of nature—is the life we save.

Holy God, this day and all days, may my road be to true life, and my choice be the life of God—your life.

Readings:
Deuteronomy 30:15-20;
Psalms 1;
Luke 9:22-25

Friday, February 19

Is such the fast that I choose . . . to lie in sackcloth and ashes? . . . Is not this the fast that I choose: to loose the bonds of injustice, . . . to share your bread with the hungry . . . ? —*Is 58:5-7*

Lord, I thank you for these early, bonus days of Lent, grace-time to shift into gear for the serious business of Lent.

So, what about this fasting business, Lord? You seem to say that true fasting is more a matter of the heart than of food, that fasting is not meant to separate me from things, from others, but to involve and connect me . . .

—not just not to eat,
   but also to share my bread with the poor;
—not just to refrain from something,
   but to do something better;
—not just to be a little uncomfortable,
   but to make someone else more comfortable;
—not just to restrain myself,
   but to set another free.

Definitely a challenge, Lord!

How can I shelter, embrace, share my bread with others today . . . so that my light can "break forth like the dawn"? (Is 58:8).

Readings: Isaiah 58:1-9a; Psalms 51; Matthew 9:14-15

Saturday, February 20

How many times had Levi (Matthew) read Psalm 86 and been comforted by its words:

. . . you, O Lord, are a God merciful and gracious, slow to anger and abounding in steadfast love and faithfulness. Turn to me and be gracious to me. . . . —*vss 15-16*

Now he sees the gentle Jesus turn his eyes to him, and Levi recognizes the look. It is not a passing glance. Jesus really sees Levi, not the Levi that others see and judge and condemn, but his inner heart and soul, filled with longing for acceptance and forgiveness . . . longings unclear to Levi himself.

If Jesus really sees Levi, Levi really sees Jesus. This Jesus is "the proof of God's favor" for whom the psalmist, and Levi, pray. From Jesus flows the strength that Levi needs to leave all the past behind to follow Jesus.

In these reflective days of Lent, we may sense vague regrets drifting in from our past, perhaps more troubling because they are so vague. The gospel tells us that in Jesus' look is all the strength we need to leave them all behind, for good.

Then you shall call, and the Lord will answer, you shall cry for help, and he will say, "Here I am." —*Is 58:9*

Readings: Isaiah 58:9-14; Psalms 86; Luke 5:27-32

First Sunday of Lent
February 21

Alas, O Lord,
Why can I not be satisfied?
The gifts of life and living do gratify,
But Eve-like and perverse
I desire to be made wise in my own conceits.
Why do I not perceive the craft of my private serpents
Who twist your precepts of love into fruits, forbidden
tantalizing?

O Lord, ". . . teach me wisdom in my secret heart. . . .
Put a new and right spirit within me. . . .
Sustain in me a willing spirit." (Ps 51:6-12)

Lent has but begun. My secret devils know how to tempt me.
Lord, let your humility arm me against stony pride,
intellectual, judgmental;
Let your fast curb my carnal appetites;
Let your fidelity shame my laggard faith,
That I may not only echo your words but strive honestly
to follow them.

> *Today, I will make a sincere effort to examine my conscience with a strong resolve to uproot those pet sins that so far have resisted correction and conversion.*

Readings: Genesis 2:7-9, 3:1-7; Psalms 51; Romans 5:12-19; Matthew 4:1-11

Monday, February 22
Chair of Saint Peter

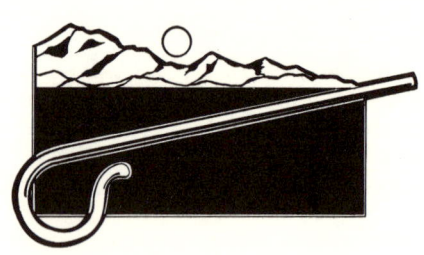

... tend the flock of God that is in your charge. ...
—1 Pt 5:2
The Lord is my shepherd, I shall not want.
—Ps 23:1
... "But who do you say that I am?"
—Mt 16:15

Powerful words to read—even more powerful words to pray.

How often, in my daily life, am I asked the above question?
  Maybe not in these words, but in words similar to them.
Does my life witness the answer
  that I profess in my quiet moments of prayer?

The only gospel that many people, in the flock I meet each day,
  may ever read is the life that they see me living.

      Am I caring enough to shepherd well?

Let me take special note of how my life lived this day will say who you are, Lord Jesus!

Readings: 1 Peter 5:1-4; Psalms 23; Matthew 16:13-19

Tuesday, February 23

This first week of Lent, we are encouraged by the Word of God today:

For as the rain and the snow come down from heaven, and do not return there until they have watered the earth . . . so shall my word be that goes out from my mouth; it shall not return to me empty, but shall accomplish that which I purpose, and succeed in the thing for which I sent it. —*Is 55:10-11*

God invites us into deeper conversation each Lent—to let go of our image of renewal, or holiness, or perfection, and to really listen and respond to God's own plans for us. Today's gospel even suggests our part of the conversation: "Our Father in heaven, hallowed be your name. Your kingdom come. Your will be done. . . . Give us this day our daily bread. And forgive us our debts, as we also have forgiven our debtors" (Mt 6: 9-12).

God both suggests the conversation and provides the blueprint for living a holy life. We need to have a close, personal relationship with God and to trust in God's care, spiritually and materially. This care is what we need to live a truly human life. The heart of this life is the recognition that God will always forgive us. We, then, must forgive one another.

O Abba, your prodigal love for me is so awe-some. If only I let you take charge of my life, all will be well. Gift me with ears that are opened to your word and a heart eager to respond to your invitation to deeper life, this day.

Readings: Isaiah 55:10-11; Psalms 34; Matthew 6:7-15

Wednesday, February 24

Create in me a clean heart, O God, and put a new and right spirit within me. *—Ps 51:10*

Today's psalm is a plea for mercy and forgiveness—a desire to be made whole. It is a prayer to be rooted in a new spirit . . . a time to change our hearts of stone into hearts of love. Whenever I pray Psalm 51, the image of water comes to my mind. We use water for cleaning, cooking, refreshment, relaxation and enjoyment. Lent is a time for inner cleansing and renewal. It is a time to recall God's tender mercy toward us and to be strengthened and nourished by that memory. It is a time of trust and openness, with confidence that our God will hear our plea for conversion and so, in that infinite mercy, grant us the clean heart we desire.

Merciful God, every time I come into contact with water today, I will remember your merciful forgiveness to me; and I will be reminded to forgive others, as I have been forgiven.

Readings: Jonah 3:1-10; Psalms 51; Luke 11:29-32

Thursday, February 25

I give you thanks, O Lord, with my whole heart; . . . On the day I called, you answered me. . . . —*Ps 138:1, 3*

How do I show my thanks to God? Not, "How *can* I show my thanks?" but "How *do* I?" Lent is a time to evaluate my life, to reflect on substituting certain attitudes and making necessary adjustments.

Celebrating is a way of thanking God for the graces and blessings given to us. When I hear good news, I frequently respond, "Thank God." Often, this is rote, spontaneous, without thinking. Today I will be more attentive to my words.

My daily prayer gives me the opportunity to express praise and thanksgiving; yet I want my actions to reflect my gratitude to God. The manner in which I forgive others is a good way of thanking God for the many times I am forgiven.

Lord, today and every day, help me to give thanks to you with my heart and my life.

Readings: Esther C:12, 14-16, 23-25; Psalms 138; Matthew 7:7-12

Friday, February 26

Out of the depths. . . .
—Ps 130:1

Out of the depths . . . I call . . .
    I need to hear your voice.
    I need to know that you will listen to my cry.
    I need to know that you will hold me fast.
    I need to know that you will never abandon me.
Out of the depths, oh my soul, I call . . . and you answer. . . .
    I know your love will sustain me.
    I know you will be near.
Out of the depths . . .
    In the deepest recesses of my soul you are there
        even before I am aware of your presence.
    You are there and that is all I need.
    You are there.
Out of the depths . . .
    Unless I forgive, be reconciled with myself, find peace,
        realize that holding on to anger or despair destroys me,
    I find myself in prison.
    I cannot get out—ever—unless I find peace by making peace.
    Unless I find it in my heart to forgive.

*Today I will reflect on a time when I was at my lowest.
I will recall what/who sustained me
and what I learned along
the way.*

Readings: Ezekiel 18:21-28;
Psalms 130; Matthew
5:20-26

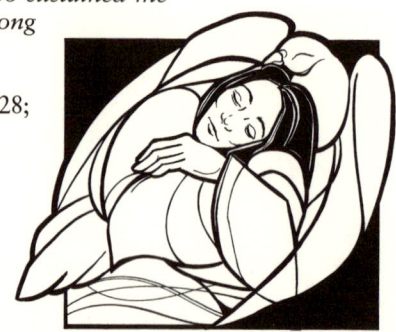

Saturday, February 27

Jesus says to us,

> "Love your enemies and pray for those who persecute you. . . ." —Mt 5:44

He wishes that we set no bounds to our love, just as our heavenly Father sets none.

As I reflect on your words, my Jesus—God, I must say thank you for your limitless gifts of grace. You continually come to my rescue so that I may live out your covenant, your commands. I have failed you numberless times, yet your graces flow in torrents over me so that I may respond to you and to my neighbor.

Teach me, O loving God, to live each day in grateful love for all your mercies.

Readings: Deuteronomy 26:16-19; Psalms 119; Matthew 5:43-48

Second Sunday of Lent
February 28

. . . "Go from your country and your kindred and your father's house to the land that I will show you." —*Gn 12:1*

There is much meaning here for me. I cannot help thinking . . . yes, I did just that as a thirteen-year-old, when I entered the high school of the Sisters of Charity. Out of this, I find great depth of meaning in Paul's letter to Timothy: ". . . God . . . called us with a holy calling, . . . according to his own purpose and grace . . . revealed through the appearing of our Savior Christ Jesus, who abolished death and brought life and immortality to light through the gospel" (2 Tm 1:8-10). How true this is of my life and, yes, of the lives of all of us who call ourselves Christian . . . a holy calling, the gift of God's grace, the fullness of life.

As Peter said to Jesus, "Lord, it is good for us to be here . . ." (Mt 17:4). I must say to the Lord, "Fifty-five years and no regrets!" Hopefully, each one of us can say the same of the way of life we have chosen to follow. If questions arise, perhaps we can ask Jesus to come and touch us with those words of comfort found in today's gospel: "Get up and do not be afraid" (Mt 17:7).

Jesus, help me to live each day, keeping in my heart the prayer of the psalmist: "Our soul waits for the Lord; he is our help and shield. Our heart is glad in him, because we trust in his holy name" (Ps 33:20-21).

Readings: Genesis 12:1-4a; Psalms 33; 2 Timothy 1:8b-10; Matthew 17:1-9

Monday, March 1

"Forgive, and you will be forgiven. . . ."
—Lk 6:37

Dearest Jesus . . . how often I say those words in the Our Father, the prayer you taught us to say. Yet, how often are they only words? You have heard me say, "Help me, O God, my savior; deliver me and pardon my sins." But have these words, too, become just words, or do they come from the depths of my heart?

Lord, you forgive; show me how to forgive as you do—with no strings attached. Show me the way so that I may be filled with compassion. In my prayer today, I will search my heart for the true meaning of this all-powerful message and pray the words of the psalmist:

**Help us, O God our salvation,
for the glory of your name;
deliver us, and forgive our sins. . . .**
—Ps 79:9

Readings: Daniel 9:4b-10; Psalms 79; Luke 6:36-38

Tuesday, March 2

"... you have but one master, the Messiah."
—Mt 23:10 (NAB)

How happy we can be to realize anew that you are our only master, Jesus. Help us to live that realization more fully these days of Lent. So many people and things attempt to rival your prime place in our lives. We can be misled and mastered by false teachers, by envy, by greed, by materialism and consumerism. When we move in the direction of these distractions, guide us gently back to you, our only master—the Messiah.

Today, I will look carefully at my life and see if I truly can claim you, Jesus, as my only Lord and Master. If I see a rival, help me to uproot it, and enthrone you once more as the first in my heart.

Readings: Isaiah 1:10, 16-20; Psalms 50; Matthew 23:1-12

Wednesday, March 3

". . . just as the Son of Man came not to be served but to serve, and to give his life a ransom for many." —*Mt 20:28*

Jesus speaks to the fact that he came to be a servant of all, and that what is asked of him is the supreme sacrifice of his life. The price for his life is spoken of, not in terms of monetary value, but the value that his life had for others—how his life's sacrifice would impact on the lives of others. His life brought life. His actions bring freedom to those who choose it—today.

I ponder these words and wonder how the actions, words, omissions of my life affect the lives of others. Jesus' life was not self-centered, with the focus on, "What will I get from this?" Rather, his was a life that was other-centered. His outstretched arms on the cross were truly symbolic of his entire life . . . one that embraced others.

Jesus, help me to be mindful of others today. Give me what I need so that my words and actions may bring life, love and freedom wherever it is needed.

Readings: Jeremiah 18:18-20; Psalms 31; Matthew 20:17-28

Thursday, March 4

Blessed are they who trust in the Lord. . . .
—Jer 17:7

As I prayerfully reflect this Lent, I ask myself: in whom, in what do I trust? Do I put my trust in money? The rich man in today's gospel must have been so consumed with money and pleasure that he completely overlooked Lazarus, the poor beggar at his door. Perhaps my trust lies in possessing power, or having powerful friends. Or do I trust in popularity and seek to be well liked, no matter what it takes? While riches, power and popularity are not bad in themselves, do I want them to be my priorities?

Rather, am I not called to trust totally in the God who loves me? Should I not rely mainly on the power of prayer, building a relationship with God? St. Vincent de Paul, who never overlooked the poor, encourages us to entrust ourselves to God's provident care: "We must abandon ourselves to God as a little child does to its nurse. . . . We should then have the same confidence in Divine Providence seeing that God takes care of all that concerns us just as a nursing mother takes care of her baby."

Today I shall examine where I place my trust. . . .
Loving God, draw me closer to you!

Readings: Jeremiah 17:5-10; Psalms 1; Luke 16:19-31

Friday, March 5

"'The stone that the builders rejected has become the cornerstone.'" —Mt 21:42

Joseph—the dreamer, the innocent—is the symbol of power to his brothers, who vie for their father's love. But Joseph's power is not created by himself; and so rejection comes from an unexpected source—his siblings—those who were supposed to know him so well.

Yet Joseph becomes a cornerstone. Rough and jagged in his brothers' eyes, he is worn to smooth, gentle curves by time and a different environment. He becomes, unknowingly, a pivotal point of interior goodness, wisdom and generosity to those who discover him. His strength is his loving compassion toward those he serves.

We are cornerstones to those we encounter in our homes and workplaces. Our strength and endurance come when we recognize our rejection—our rough and jagged place—and use it to become a quiet point of wisdom and strength for others.

Lord, help me to identify a rough edge in my life today, and to put it under your loving gaze to enable your healing smoothness.

Readings: Genesis 37:3-4, 12-13a, 17b-28; Psalms 105; Matthew 21:33-43, 45-46

Saturday, March 6

. . . we had to celebrate and rejoice, because this brother of yours was dead and has come to life; he was lost and has been found.
—*Lk 15:32*

One day, as I was reading this account of the gospel, I realized how my thoughts were those of the older son, at times. How often have I heard of someone who lived free and easy, spending money wastefully, hurting others, even committing crime, yet being welcomed to a civil gathering, because he or she made a large donation to charity? And, truthfully, my thoughts would not be very pleasant.

"Just look at the kind of lives they lead," I'd say to myself, "and now they get the red carpet treatment in their honor!" Other times I've found myself saying, "I'm working day in and day out, getting no recognition, while this one goes off and has a good time!" Or, "She makes one little speech and gets applause that could bring the house down!"

As I read the words of the father to the older son, I realized how wrong I was. Does not God assure me that "everything I have is yours?" How the words of today's gospel took on new meaning for me!

Today, I will spend some time reflecting on the words of the father to the older son and listen to what else God may be saying to my heart.

Readings: Micah 7:14-15, 18-20; Psalms 103; Luke 15:1-3, 11-32

Third Sunday of Lent
March 7

Today's scriptures speak of journey—a journey from brokenness to wholeness—a life's journey. And though the way is often unclear and almost never linear, there are some signs that serve to guide me and keep me moving. Will you travel with me?

My journey begins in Exodus, the desert of my lack of trust in a loving Creator, where my spirit falters and I thirst for a reason to hope. I am stuck in this place. But a sign—the psalmist's call to open my heart and to hear God's voice. Could it be that my *openness* to journey is more important than knowing my destination?

God of all possibilities, help me to be open to the new and unexpected in my life!

Paul's letter offers me reassurance . . . hope does not disappoint . . . (Rom 5:5). I am loved. God's love freely given provides a respite in my journey and a stimulus to continue. With a hope fueled by this love, I move forward. I strive to recognize God's gift in my journey. I pray for the courage of the Samaritan woman who went public about this gift, and whose testimony opened others to the experience of God's love.

Thank you, God; you have brought me from dry land to living water . . . let the journey continue.

Readings: Exodus 17:3-7; Psalms 95; Romans 5:1-2, 5-8; John 4:5-42

Monday, March 8

"... no prophet is accepted in his own native place."
—Lk 4:24 (NAB)

We all feel the same—no matter what our vocation, job, position or accomplishments. We want, or at least expect, to be accepted, heard, admired and listened to as the adults we have become by those who knew us in the becoming—in our own place. But it just doesn't happen.

Jesus learned this early in his ministry. He knew the Hebrew scriptures and understood clearly why Elijah and Elisha worked their miracles outside their community. Yet Jesus still tried to go to his own place . . . to the synagogue, only to hear, "Is not this Joseph's son?" It had to hurt as it hurts us when we can't use our talents in our own place.

Perhaps this hurtful side of ministry is necessary to push us "out of the womb" toward a world that is in need of us. Perhaps acceptance by those "outside" breaks down walls of ignorance, discrimination and fear . . . ours and theirs.

We are sent, and we must go. We must leave home. We must form communities of faith, not blood, with strangers. In this manner, we preach the gospel and have the gospel preached to us.

Today, let me look anew at those around me. Am I hearing the Word of God they are bringing to me? Are they hearing the Word I am bringing to them?

Readings: 2 Kings 5:1-15a; Psalms 42; Luke 4:24-30

Tuesday, March 9

> . . . Azariah stood still in the fire and he prayed aloud.
> *—Dn 3:25*

It is so easy to praise God and to bless the Lord when all is well in my life:
- when the sun shines.
- when my work goes well.
- when losses are few.
- when relationships are comfortable.
- when my agenda and my time are my own.
- when peace reigns in my heart.

But in FIRE, God?
- when someone distrusts?
- when losses of any kind occur?
- when mystery confronts me?
- when I feel betrayed?
- when the flames engulf me?

Ah! Then I am more likely only to plead for deliverance, or even to gripe, than to praise and bless! Grant me a contrite soul, O God, a humbled spirit acceptable to you.

Today I will praise and bless God for ALL the happenings in my life; and I will express gratitude to those who help strengthen my faith when I am in the fire.

Readings: Daniel 3:25, 34-43; Psalms 25; Matthew 18:21-35

Wednesday, March 10

For what other great nation has a god so near to it as the Lord our God is whenever we call to him? —*Dt 4:7*

The sacred scriptures vividly portray the closeness of God to Israel, the people of the Covenant, the chosen people. Is not God still closer to us, Jew and Gentile, people of the New Covenant, sealed in the blood of Jesus Christ? Our Lord Jesus Christ, the Word made flesh, offered himself to make reparation for the sins of all people of every time and place, of every race and nation, of every color and language.

Every time the mass is celebrated, Christ's one, sacrificial offering for the forgiveness of sins is made sacramentally present. I can unite with that offering. My reception of his holy body and blood in the communion of the mass deepens my loving union with Christ and intensifies the divine life within me. It strengthens me in responding to his call to continue his mission so that all may be one in Christ.

How do I fulfill my responsibility to reveal Christ's love and communicate his teaching? What cultural prejudices and insensitivity impede my fulfilling that responsibility?

Readings: Deuteronomy 4:1, 5-9; Psalms 147; Matthew 5:17-19

Thursday, March 11

Others, to test him [Jesus], kept demanding from him a sign from heaven.
—Lk 11:16

How often, my God, have I also asked for a sign! On one occasion, I was even so bold as to specify the kind of sign I wanted.

Confusion, turmoil, decision making are part of life. Making a choice can be difficult when the pros and cons appear to be of equal value. Sometimes I am paralyzed. I cannot or do not want to choose—fearful of the unknown, of new demands, of change, of possible failure and even of possible success. And so I ask you, my God, to choose; a sign from you will be all I need.

Why do I test you? Why am I blind to those signs and miracles within and around me already? You are present to me in your Word, in the eucharist, in the whisperings of your Spirit and in the companions with whom I journey. How slow I am to know your ways! How weak my trust!

May the signs of your love and the gifts of your peace—the fullness of life—be all I seek today.

Readings: Jeremiah 7:23-28; Psalms 95; Luke 11:14-23

Friday, March 12

We are called to prayerful, effective conversion today as we reflect on the words of the prophet Hosea and those of Jesus. Especially significant is that both Hosea and Jesus invite us to consider the larger community. Hosea addresses the whole of Israel to change their ways. Jesus challenges all of us to love God and neighbor, bringing us to the question, "Who is my neighbor?"

"Return . . . to the Lord, your God. . . . Take words with you and return to the Lord . . ." (Hos 14:1-2) was Hosea's call to conversion. Perhaps we need to look at the words we take to God in our prayers today. Would God respond to our prayer differently because we have more carefully reflected upon our words? Would our reflection help us to hear God differently?

We hear Jesus speak the two great laws of love, words that we have known for many years: love of God and love of neighbor. Our conversion in response to Jesus precludes false gods, and our love of neighbor includes the dispossessed, the homeless, those who are foreign to us, not usually included in our circles of acquaintances.

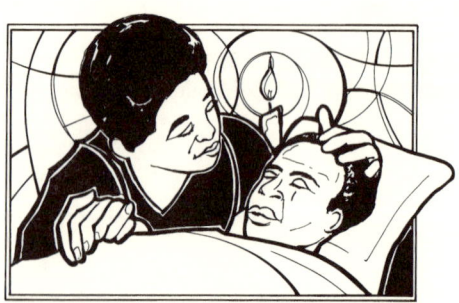

Today, I will reflect on my relationships and how I am being called to conversion in my life.

Readings: Hosea 14:2-10; Psalms 81; Mark 12:28b-34

Saturday, March 13

Have mercy on me, O God, according to your steadfast love; according to your abundant mercy blot out my transgressions.
—Ps 51:1

Lent is a time for fasting and prayer, accompanied by almsgiving and penance. If our fasting is rooted in our prayer, then our relationship with God is rooted in our hearts, not just on our lips. Our words are transformed by love. We can trust that God will answer us, when we place no conditions on what God can accomplish.

In the gospel according to Luke, the Pharisee mouths empty words and places conditions for his prayer to God. The tax collector, believing in God's mercy and love, simply asks for forgiveness. This servant is awed by God's love for him, and so finds himself immersed in the heart of God's love—divine forgiveness.

This way to God is also available to me. God welcomes me and renews me like the spring rain that waters the earth. God's request for me is simple and clear—my steadfast love in return for God's.

This day, help me to renew my promise to be loyal in my love for you, merciful God, and to accept your gracious love and grace without conditions.

Readings: Hosea 6:1-6; Psalms 51; Luke 18:9-14

Fourth Sunday of Lent
March 14

"Not as man sees does God see, because man sees the appearance but the Lord looks into the heart." *—1 Sm 16:7 (NAB)*

The bright sun gives no warning of the clouds that will later fill the sky. The mail brings unexpected news of the death of a friend. The young couple in the upstairs apartment have separated; they seemed the perfect pair. Things are often not what they appear to be.

Do I simply go along looking at surface signs, not paying attention or taking time to read the deeper significance they may hold? What of those who enter my life—the persons with whom I live or work? Do I take them for granted, too?

Is it only making school lunches, sharing carpools, doing the laundry, finishing the report for work, clearing off my desk at the end of the day? Or do I gaze at a sleeping child and see the gift of life?

How do I respond when someone asks for help, or when a knock on the door jars my concentration? How do I view the jobless, the homeless, those of different color or language? Do I judge my appearance, or do I recognize all whom I encounter as brothers and sisters in Christ? Do I look into the human heart and find the heart of Christ?

Today, I will take time to discover the many ways Christ enters my life.

Readings: 1 Samuel 16:1b, 6-7, 10-13a; Psalms 23; Ephesians 5:8-14; John 9:1-41

Monday, March 15

The man believed the word that Jesus spoke to him and started on his way. —*Jn 4:50*

Trusting in God's word is a difficult challenge for me when I experience events taking a different turn from what I had expected. I tend to panic and then silently hope the situation will reverse itself. Each day I am asked to let go and to trust in the word of Jesus. Can I do this? Is it within my grasp? What of those moments that seem just too difficult? These are the real tests of my trust.

For me, Jesus is the Word through which God speaks. This Word must mean my whole life if I am to be truly his follower. At times, God's Word seems to lack clarity. These are the times I must trust and intuit with greater awareness exactly what the Word is saying for me. I must be a person who truly hears the Word of God and keeps it in my heart. I must act in such a way that others will break open the Word and share it with me.

Father, there are times when too many words bombard me, so that I fail to hear your Word. Help me to quietly discern your Word for me on my journey; then I, too, like the trusting father, will be able to start for home.

Today I will read a brief passage from scripture, slowly, and try to discern God's message for me.

Readings: Isaiah 65:17-21; Psalms 30; John 4:43-54

Tuesday, March 16

One man was there who had been ill for thirty-eight years. When Jesus saw him lying there . . . he said to him, "Do you want to be made well?" . . . "Sir, I have no one to put me into the pool. . . ." Jesus said to him, "Stand up . . . and walk."
—Jn 5:5-8

Is it possible that, for a number of years, someone has been in the same place every day in need of a helping hand, and I am blind to it? Jesus asks a simple question: "Do you want to be well?" Is it possible that no one except Jesus spoke to this man?

Jesus' words speak loudly to me today about what Jesus values. I hear him ask me, "What do you want?" Dare I say to him, "I want your values to be my values"? That means I would have to open my eyes and look at those around me with the compassionate eyes of Jesus. That means I would have to say to them, truly from my heart, "May I help you . . . may I help you get up and walk?"

Jesus, let me not be blind to anyone I meet today. Help me to see them through your eyes. Give me the courage to speak the first words of care and concern, in imitation of you.

Readings: Ezekiel 47:1-9, 12; Psalms 46; John 5:1-16

Wednesday, March 17

"Can a woman forget her nursing child, or show no compassion for the child in her womb? Even should she forget, I will never forget you."
—Is 49:15 (NAB)

There is a child in each of us who longs to hear the words, "I love you." This is especially true when it comes from someone close to us. In the words of Isaiah, our compassionate God is letting us know how loved we truly are. God uses the image of a mother nurturing her daughter or son, saying to us, "I love you even more than a mother does her baby. I will never forget you!"

As I struggle along in these last weeks of Lent, conscious that my good intentions of Ash Wednesday have been somewhat forgotten, God's word reawakens those initial Lenten promises, and stirs my heart to respond.

Jesus, as I live this day, I will carry these words with me. I will look for your holy face in the faces of my brothers and sisters and . . . I will remember you.

Readings: Isaiah 49:8–15; Psalms 145; John 5:17–30

Thursday, March 18

Today's scripture speaks to me about my unfaithfulness to God! In John 5:44 (NAB), I experience the words: "How can you believe, when you accept praise from one another and do not seek the praise that comes from the only God?"

Lent draws me back to an awareness of my faults and omissions in daily life . . . how I tend to become discouraged and to complain about my misfortune in life, feeling left to deal in isolation when, in reality, I look only to those who also grumble and complain.

Today, I have the opportunity to refocus my mind and heart and, in a spirit of repentance, redirect my vision toward the will of God.

Faithful God, I pray that I may join my spirit this day with your will. Help me to listen attentively to your call.

So the Lord relented in the punishment he had threatened to inflict on his people.
—Ex 32:14 (NAB)

Readings:
Exodus 32:7-14; Psalms 106; John 5:31-47

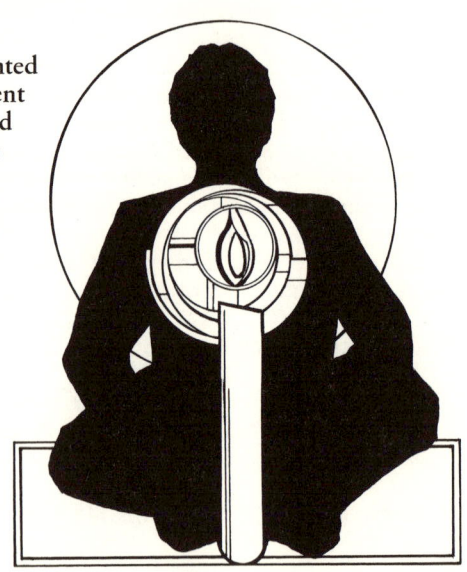

Friday, March 19
Saint Joseph

Then he [Jesus] went down with them and came to Nazareth, and was obedient to them. —*Lk 2:51*

Why must my meditation today take me down to Nazareth when I have been plodding for weeks toward Golgatha? Because you, Joseph—the quiet man, the obedient, caring, humble man—would have me stop and reflect on your part in the great plan of salvation.

In obedience to the angel, you took Mary as your spouse and gave the child she carried his legal name. In obedience to the emperor, you traveled with Mary to Bethlehem, where the child was destined to be born. Another command, and you fled by night with mother and child to the safety of exile, then back to Galilee to establish a home for your family.

I search the scriptures for a single word that you spoke. I find none. You live in the WORD as a quiet man of action, as protector of Jesus and Mary, dedicating yourself to a life of loving them. And God's Son, on the threshold of manhood, goes down from the temple in Jerusalem to Nazareth to live in obedience to you and Mary.

Lord Jesus, let me learn from your Joseph all the virtues you loved in him. Help me to imitate him in his dedication to a life lived in love for you.

Readings: 2 Samuel 7:4-5a, 12-14a; Psalms 89; Romans 4:13, 16-18, 22; Luke 2:41-51

Saturday, March 20

Put an end to evil, uphold the good; you test our hearts, God of right and truth. —*Ps 7:10 (ICEL)*

Prophets make us see things as they really are. Jeremiah recalls the words of the psalmist lamenting in a time of persecution. If only God would play the just judge and provide saving help in the time of distress.

God has surely tested our hearts, our minds, our sensitivities, perhaps our very faith. News broadcasts bring vividly, before our eyes and ears, acts of cruelty and inhumanity . . . in our neighborhoods and across the globe. Isn't God paying attention? When will the good and gracious Creator reach down and punish the mean-spirited, the conceivers of evil, the troublemakers of this world? And even my personal enemies?

God of glory and light, I know it is important for me to recognize that even in an unfair world you remain the God of right and truth. Your son, Jesus, one of us— lived with uncertainty, criticism, denial, abandonment, a cruel and unjust death. Even Jesus sought relief from persecution, all the while holding on to hope. Why, then, should I want things to be different for me?

As I am put to the test daily and struggle to remain faithful, what keeps me anchored in the sure and certain hope that God will not abandon me?

Readings: Jeremiah 11:18-20; Psalms 7; John 7:40-53

Fifth Sunday of Lent
March 21

For me, today's readings are filled with the promise of redemption and salvation. Psalm 130 helps me to call upon God's mercy from the depths of my sinfulness. My surety is that there is forgiveness for me.

In the readings from both Ezekiel and John, the image of the opening of graves is powerful. I can see Jesus opening the grave of my sinfulness and loosening me from the weight of my guilt. How good and gracious is the God who inspires me to repent, who hears my heartfelt cry for forgiveness and assures me of great love, acceptance and redemption.

Today, each time I look at my watch, I will proclaim the goodness of the Lord and his steadfast love. And I will praise him for his saving love in my life.

Readings: Ezekiel 37:12-14; Psalms 130; Romans 8:8-11; John 11:1-45

Monday, March 22

To stand alone before a crowd is a soul-stirring experience. It could be a moment of triumph, of control, of jubilation—the world is ours. But to stand alone and condemned before a hostile, curious crowd must be terrifying.

Jesus' enemies interrupt his teaching by bringing in a woman who was guilty of a crime that was punishable by death, under the law. These men were out to trap Jesus—to force him to speak against the law of Moses and in favor of his own philosophy of forgiveness. Slowly and deliberately, Jesus responds to their condemnation; they are shamed into silence and they disappear with the crowd.

Only God can know all the past events and the particular, unique circumstances of life that have brought a person to a present situation. Whether one stands innocent of an accusation but helpless before an evil power or strong foe, or another be guilty of breaking a law, God demonstrates an unconditional, incredible love. Jesus rescues the innocent and forgives the guilty in his own time and own way.

The fact that I strive to be a law-abiding person is not a reason to justify myself or to accept salvation as my due. It is God's merciful justice that saves every soul created out of love.

When I stand before you, Lord Jesus, with only your eyes upon me, I find that I must always forgive or be forgiven. I ask pardon for my sins and forgive anyone who judges me unjustly.

Readings: Daniel 13:1-9, 15-17, 19-30, 33-62; Psalms 23; John 8:1-11

Tuesday, March 23

"... the one who sent me is with me...."
—Jn 8:29

As we move toward the end of this Lenten journey, it is inevitable that we begin to tire and feel discouraged. The road seems a bit too long these days, and there are a hundred reasons why we feel we can back away from our Lenten disciplines and resolutions. Yet today's readings prod us to keep the bigger picture in mind.

God sustains us in the good times and in the difficult times; God does not leave us alone. Jesus declared, strongly, his conviction that God was with him, even as he was challenged by the authorities of his day. Living in God's loving presence, we are challenged each day to ask ourselves if we are truly living in a way that gives witness to our beliefs. Our age cries for signs of compassion and for those who work for justice in the light of the gospel.

Today, I will intentionally pause at early morning, midday and evening to recall God's loving presence and to recommit myself to the journey.

Readings: Numbers 21:4–9; Psalms 102; John 8:21–30

WEDNESDAY, MARCH 24

"... there is no place in you for my word."
—Jn 8:37

Yes, Lord, I know what you are saying. It is spring cleaning time, and my house is not in order. How do I let so much clutter build up, clutter that acts as a wall to keep you at a distance from me? Even knowing that there is no room for your Word in my heart, I keep on piling up the chaff with the wheat, the weeds with the flowers, the work with the prayer.

Please, Lord, let your Spirit breathe away the chaff. Be the Gardener working at my side, pulling up the weeds and reworking the soil, so that the flowers may bloom with full beauty. Teach me again, O patient Tutor of my soul, how to make my work be my prayer. Teach me how to plant your Word right into the wall I have erected, so that as your truth grows strong in me once again, I may become free of those restraints that are so effective in keeping me at a distance from you.

"... and the truth will make you free."
—Jn 8:32

Readings: Daniel 3:14-20, 91-92, 95; Daniel 3:52-56; John 8:31-42

Thursday, March 25

Greetings, favored one!
The Lord is with you. . . .
Do not be afraid. . . .
    —Lk 1:28, 30

Mary encounters a God of surprises.
Confused and troubled by the angel's words,
She pauses and ponders them deeply in her heart.

Gabriel comforts her again as "favored one,"
Announcing that she will bear the Son of the Most High
Named Jesus, the Holy One who will be great
Presiding over the kingdom of God,
And the people of God forever.

Mary is puzzled and explicitly states,
"How can this be, since I have no relations with a man?"
God, through Gabriel, reassures her and urges trust,
Promising her empowerment and protection.

Having listened, pondered and prayed,
Mary proclaims her oneness with God,
Becoming a vessel of the living God
And filling her heart with acts of faith and love.

O loving God . . . Jesus, born of Mary, enable me to fill my heart with acts of love and faith today, and to respond positively to the incomprehensible, the impossible and the surprises of my life. Grant this liberating spirit to those who clamor for it, and to me. Amen.

Readings: Isaiah 7:10-14, 8:10; Psalms 40; Hebrews 10:4-10; Luke 1:26-38

Friday, March 26

God's way is unerring; the Lord's promise is tried and true.... *—Ps 18:31 (NAB)*

God, our God—as winter wanes, I often wonder if new life and warmth will ever come. But deep in my heart, I never doubt the constant, recurring promise of spring. Yet I often find it difficult to abandon myself to you, in spite of the promise that your way is love, truth, freedom and light.

Help me to move beyond my lack of trust to allow you to possess me, to accept that there is no other way. Give me the grace to believe in you without doubt, as our ancestors did when they sang in joy, trial and darkness, "Your way is unerring, your promise is tried and true." Give me a heartfelt faith that you are with me, with us, to support, strengthen, inspire and guide. Help me to do what only pleases you—loving and serving others with a profound trust in your promise.

O Lord, help me to accept your way completely. Strengthen me to love you so passionately that I will seek only your will.

Readings: Jeremiah 20:10-13; Psalms 18; John 10:31-42

Saturday, March 27

. . . You know nothing at all! You do not understand. . . .
—Jn 11:49-50

It often strikes me that I do not understand! What is it about Lent that I find so difficult to grasp? The message is clear enough—Jesus is risen! Jesus is here! I think the conversion of Lent calls me to change my thinking, open my heart and *trust* that Jesus is here.

The Lenten theme at a local parish this year is "Road to Resurrection." I admit that, too often, I stay only on the Road to Crucifixion, concentrating on suffering. I focus on two things: I'll never be good enough for Jesus, and I am responsible for saving the world.

But the story doesn't end with suffering and death! The story ends with Jesus coming out of the tomb like a butterfly from its chrysalis—resplendent in glory, radiant with affirmation, love and acceptance. I must enter the spirit of Lent and Easter, then, by being myself—a woman created in the image and likeness of God, loved, accepted, cherished as a daughter.

God, my Creator, thank you for all the good things in my life, for talents and gifts to share with others. Today, I will affirm the gifts of a coworker or family member. I will accept my own gifts and remind myself that you are always near.

Readings: Ezekiel 37:21-28; Jeremiah 31:10-13; John 11:45-57

PASSION SUNDAY
MARCH 28

My God, my God, why have you forsaken me?
—Ps 22:1

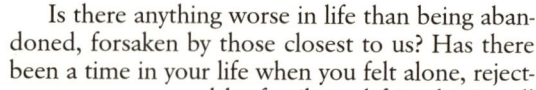

Is there anything worse in life than being abandoned, forsaken by those closest to us? Has there been a time in your life when you felt alone, rejected by family and friends? Recall that occasion, experience that feeling of loneliness, isolation or depression. Then place yourself at the foot of the cross, look up and behold your God; hear his loud cries of desolation: "Father, where are you? Why have you left me alone? I cry and you do not answer, why are you so far from me? Is there no one to deliver me from this hostility and suffering?"

The power of hell has been unleashed, but it will not prevail. The Father, who hears the cry of the poor, did not abandon his only begotten Son. There is an inner strength in Jesus, a power stronger than death . . . it is love. Love will triumph over evil and sin, desolation and abandonment! Jesus trusts in his Father and in the Father's plan for salvation. In full surrender Jesus prayed, "Not my will, but yours be done."

Let us spend time, this Holiest of Weeks, at the foot of the cross contemplating the suffering Jesus. Let us pour out our hearts in love and gratitude for his immense love for us and make our prayer the prayer of Jesus, "Father, your will be done."

Readings: Matthew 21:1-11; Isaiah 50:4-7; Psalms 22; Philippians 2:6-11; Matthew 26:14—27:66

Monday of Holy Week
March 29

"Here is my servant . . . he will bring forth justice. . . ."
—Is 42:1

These words from the prophet Isaiah continue to haunt me.

To bring forth justice
  He will not cry or lift up his voice,
  Or make it heard in the street. . . .
  —Is 42:2

How, then, do you want me to serve you?
How can I be your prophet?
How can I witness to you?
I am called to proclaim justice—to be a prophet
  To proclaim justice that goes beyond my words,
    justice that is embodied in my actions.

If it is true that actions follow being, the actions of my life will become the acts of Jesus' compassion, love and solidarity with all humanity—poor and rich, young and old, ill and well, women and men, black and white, uneducated and learned. The message of Jesus that the reign of God is for all people will be credible to the extent that I live what I proclaim.

Today, I will be grateful for the privilege to proclaim Christ's message and for the challenge to live what I proclaim.

Readings: Isaiah 42:1-7; Psalms 27; John 12:1-11

TUESDAY OF HOLY WEEK
MARCH 30

. . . Jesus was troubled in spirit, and declared, " . . . one of you will betray me." *—Jn 13:21*

On the night before his death, among the chosen twelve who had faithfully walked so long and so far with Jesus, there was betrayal—by Judas and eventually by Peter.

Betrayal is always devastating. It is accompanied by shock, disbelief, sadness and pain. And yet, in the very act of betrayal was the *redemptive moment*—the Lamb of God was slain. The sacrifice was made.

Do I fall into the Judas trap and let earthly treasures of money, prestige and power nudge me into betraying the call to live radically Christian? Do I fall into the Peter trap and pretend I am not a follower?

Pray that we never forget the promise:

". . . I will give you as a light to the nations, that my salvation may reach to the end of the earth." *—Is 49:6*

Readings: Isaiah 49:1-6; Psalms 71; John 13:21-33, 36-38

Wednesday of Holy Week
March 31

. . . "Truly I tell you, one of you will betray me."
—Mt 26:21

How much it must have pained Jesus to know that one of his closest friends was about to betray him. He had spent three years teaching his apostles and they still did not know him. One of his own, not one of his enemies, was about to hand him over.

Jesus knew Judas was the one, yet he gave him every opportunity to have a change of heart. Judas also knew, but he was so consumed with what he was about to do that he could not hear Jesus calling to him in his heart . . . calling him to return to his place among the chosen ones.

How many times a day am I so consumed with my own agenda that I fail to hear Jesus calling me to himself . . . to respond from my heart, where he offers me peace? Today, I will make every effort to attune myself to the voice of Jesus, to hear his word and to learn his way.

Readings: Isaiah 50:4-9a; Psalms 69; Matthew 26:14-25

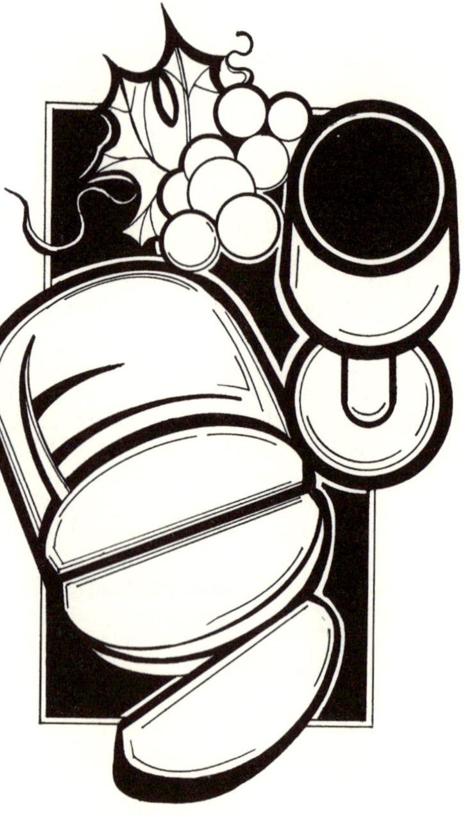

HOLY THURSDAY
APRIL 1

". . . Do this in remembrance of me."
—1 Cor 11:24

In this letter to the Corinthians, as well as in a similar passage from the gospel according to Luke, this command of Jesus, "Do this in remembrance of me," immediately follows the words of the institution of the eucharist. To "re-member," to "do this" is to make present again the action of Christ.

Authentic remembering requires imitation of Christ:

—welcoming strangers

—serving those in need

—mending tears in the fabric of community

—moving toward inclusiveness

—taking on the mind of Jesus

—participating in his suffering for the sake of others

In a community whose members do not love one another, there can be no eucharist. Ritual action alone, even with all the prescribed words and gestures, is of little value to me or to the community unless God's saving word, in its fullness, is enfleshed in the community.

Only then is eucharist possible!

How fully does my community celebrate eucharist? Do we truly do what Christ has done?

Readings: Exodus 12:1-8, 11-14; Psalms 116; 1 Corinthians 11:23-26; John 13:1-15

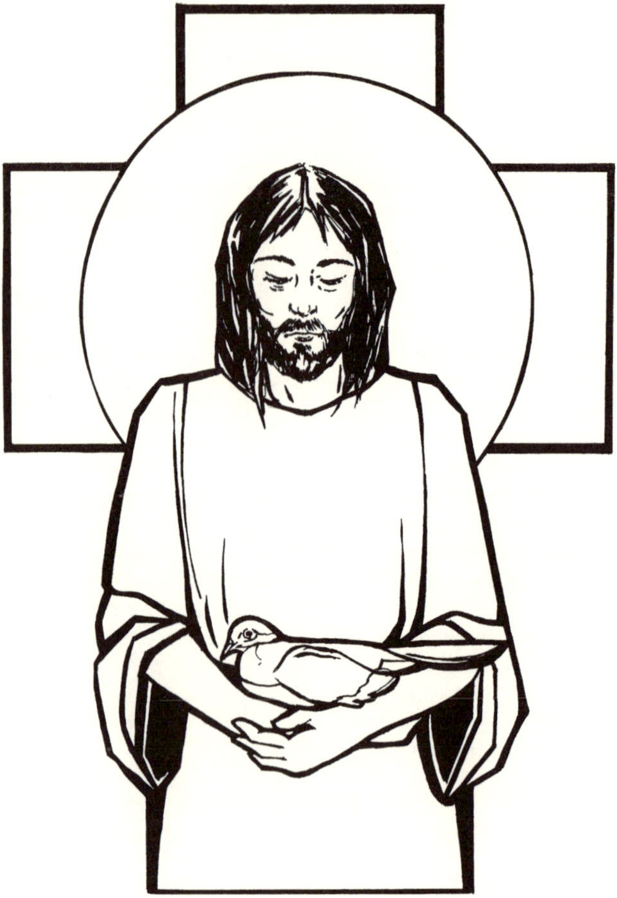

Good Friday
April 2

If we have "stayed awake" these past forty days, our Lenten journey may have surprised us with new revelations of God's love and mercy. These days have been great gifts, opened to reveal the sometimes unclaimed parts of ourselves that are masked by our own self-centeredness, righteousness and pride. We journeyed *inward,* asking forgiveness for our failings and *outward,* in service and almsgiving, desiring to make a difference in our world.

Good Friday brings us face to face with Jesus' ultimate act of surrender to his ABBA. How often I have chastised myself for not being able to trust with the faith to which the scriptures challenge me this day. It is easy to trust that the sun will rise at the dawn of a new day,

> that the stoplight will eventually turn green,
>
> that spring will bring the return of the flowers.

The level of trust that Jesus exemplifies today is calling me to believe each day that God will surely intercede in my life. I long to let the fears that bind me unwind so that I, too, may embrace with Jesus the liberation that only an Easter morn will bring to fullness.

Readings: Isaiah 52:13–53:12; Psalms 31; Hebrews 4:14-16, 5:7-9; John 18:1–19:42

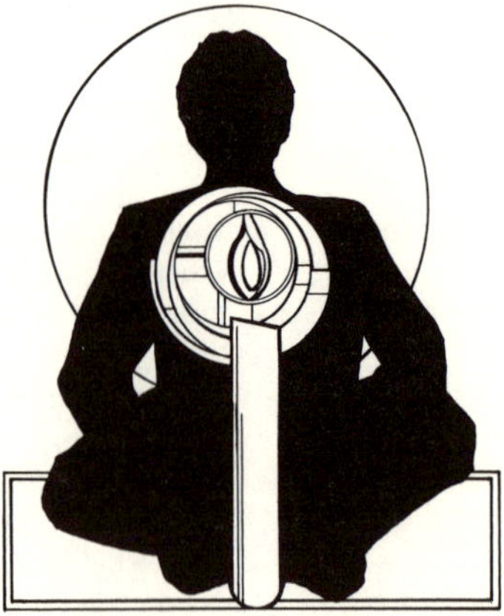

Holy Saturday
April 3

Holy Saturday seems like the loneliest day of the whole year. The altars are stripped, the musical instruments are silent, and even the eucharist is hidden away to be distributed only to the very sick. It is the kind of time we've all known in our personal lives after the death of a loved one, when we are all waiting for the final rituals to begin. The paradox is one of being filled with emptiness as we remember precious moments of a last meal, last words and, perhaps, of labored, dying breaths.

Today's vigil readings invite us to reflect on the dreams, hopes and struggles of all God's people throughout salvation history. Dorothy Day called her path on that journey *The Long Loneliness.* Today we, too, share in that long loneliness of our journey to God.

Like the holy women of the gospel, we now wait for the dawn of a new day. They waited in love and grief to anoint the body of Jesus. We wait in love and hope to greet the risen Christ.

As we join other Christians in the day-long vigil, we pray:

Keep us safe, O God; you are our hope!

Readings: Genesis: 1:1–2:2; Exodus 14:15–15:1; Isaiah 55:1-11; Psalms 42; Romans 6:3-11; Matthew 28:1-10

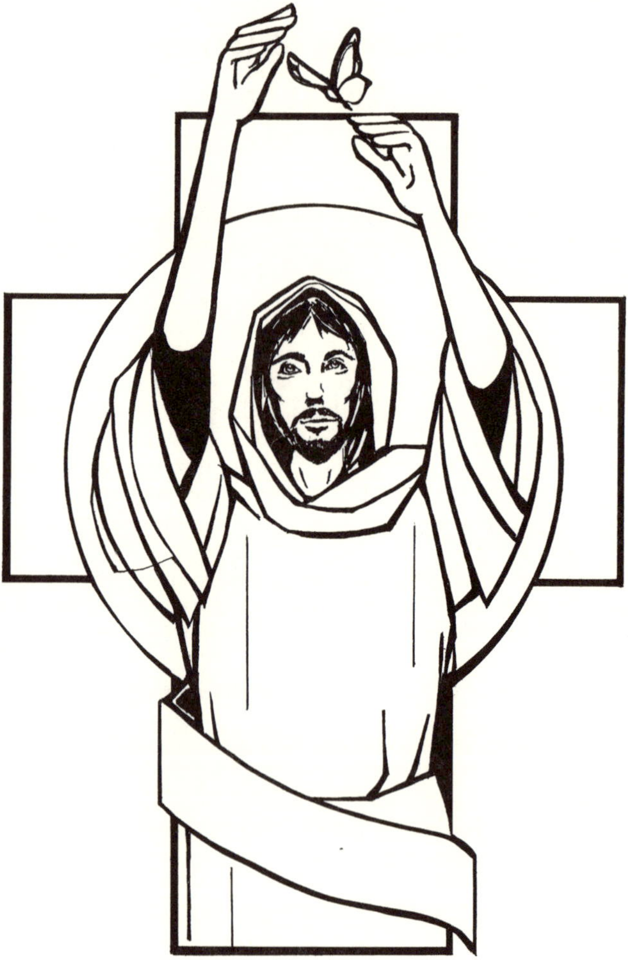

Easter Sunday
April 4

He . . . saw the linen wrappings lying there. . . .
—Jn 20:5

Jesus, saving gift of the Father,
Unwrapped and alive,
No stone or shroud or tomb of death
Could restrain the new-life impulse
Of your resurrected glory.

Hasten my steps from the empty grave
  this Easter day
To my own risen life hidden in yours.

Jettison my heart from the mire of mourning
To joyous praise in your appearing.

Choose me, too, Lord Jesus, as your
  witness
as I gather today at table,
Feasting, celebrating, marveling.
And I begin to understand

  . . . You are alive!

Readings: Acts 10:34a, 37-43; Psalms 118; Colossians 3:1-4; John 20:1-9

CONTRIBUTORS
IN ORDER OF APPEARANCE:

Sisters Ellen Dauwer, Therese Aquinas Roche, Barbara Connell, Jean Whitley, Grace Roberta McBreen, Carol Heller, Kathleen Flanagan, Maryanne Tracey, Mary Fallon, Rose Marie Padovano, Therese Dorothy Leland, Jean Cordis Mangin, Mary Cullen, Clare Mary Roden, Judy Mertz, Edna Francis Hersinger, Mary Farrell, Marie Henry, Roseann Mazzeo, Ann Stango, Bernadette Therese McCann, Hildegarde Marie Mahoney, Maureen Mylott, Mary Anne Katlack, Mary Morley, Francis Cordis Bernardo, Anne McDonald, Cecilia Burns, Julia Scanlan, Catherine Morrisett, Francis Maria Cassidy, Barbara Conroy, Anita William O'Neill, Rosemary Campbell, Maureen Shaughnessy, Alberta Keuhlen, Grace Reape, Rosemary Moynihan, Joan Repka, Regina Suplick, Frances Scarfone, Kathleen Quigley, Joan Wickers, Rosemary Smith, Roberta Feil, Mary Canavan, Cheryl France.